# BE AWESOME ON PURPOSE

## BONNIE NIEVES

EduMatch Publishing

# CONTENTS

# 1

## INTRODUCTION

### My Story

**M**y sister hated it; from the time she was an infant, she was my student. I loved school and being six years older, I felt compelled to prepare her for her upcoming journey. She progressed from being in a booster seat reciting the alphabet and counting to ten to eventually being able to sit and write sight words at her tiny wooden desk in my bedroom in front of my worn-out chalkboard. I was in my glory. Among her classmates Winnie The Pooh, Barbie, and Tiffany the dog, she was the star pupil. I remember explaining the importance of what I was teaching her as she tried to leave to go play with her Strawberry Shortcake dolls. Eventually, Strawberry and her friends were enrolled in my class along with the others.

Teaching was my calling; I felt it even on the first day of kinder-garten. My mother's recollection is clearer than mine of the day that I bounded home from the bus stop into the house. She tells me about how excited I was to tell her about my new friends and activi-ties that I could teach my sister. On that day and every first day of elementary school, she helped me fill out my reflection book. I remained steadfast in my plans; I wanted to be a teacher when I grew up.

**KINGERGARTEN** *(form image)*

NEW FRIENDS
LEANN
KAREN
SHARON
JOHNATHON

Todd
ChRISTINA — ScoTT
GARY
BARRY
TAmmy
TAmmy

ACTIVITIES

ACHIEVEMENTS

AWARDS

**WHEN I GROW UP I WANT TO BE —**

BOYS / GIRLS

☐ Fireman ☐ Astronaut ☐ Mother ☐ Airline Hostess
☐ Policeman ☐ Soldier ☐ Nurse ☐ Model
☐ Cowboy ☐ Baseball Player ☒ School Teacher ☐ Secretary

SIGNATURE BonnieMcIntyre

The gender bias of this does not go unnoticed. If I were encouraged to be a firefighter or scientist, my answer would not have been any different.

Although it seems that my path was set out before me, my road to becoming a teacher was anything but straight and narrow. The first curve was in junior high where it seemed most of my teachers did not value curiosity as much as compliance. My grades plummeted as I became disinterested and disengaged. I was ultimately labeled a trouble-student. Eyes rolled when I was introduced to my teachers in freshman year.

The Ds and Fs on my academic record are the landmarks along the path that tells the story of the importance of connecting with a teacher or not. Without the deeper learning experiences that I craved and opportunities to pursue my interests, every day I became further detached from the classroom. Eventually, there were more diversions than times I stayed the course, and my dream of being a teacher diminished along with my GPA.

\* \* \*

While working on my BS in Biology, I worked in a variety of jobs from medical assisting to insurance case management; I was always designated the preceptor for new employees. People often asked me why I wasn't taking education classes. "You're a natural,"

"This is in your blood,"

were things I heard regularly. My response was always the same; I can't be a teacher because I love learning too much. In my experience as a learner, teaching and learning did not align.

*I can't be a teacher because*
*I love learning too much.*

My career in education started as a result of months of prodding by my college career counselor as I prepared to complete my undergraduate degree. She convinced me that my fresh perspective and curiosity were needed in education. I had the honor of working with several veteran teachers over the course of five years. The lessons learned from this experience helped build the foundation of my

career. I saw teachers' various styles and paid attention to their
short- and long-term patterns. With all of their best intentions, a
persistent and comfortable cycle seemed to remain consistent and
hadn't changed much since my disappointing experience in junior
high:

1. Teacher schedules test according to report card date
2. Teacher gives notes, students take notes
3. Students take quiz
4. Teacher gives lectures, students take notes
5. Students take quiz
6. Review
7. Students take test
8. Grades go on report cards
9. Repeat

Notice the ownership here; teachers give and students take.
There was a theme of students being passive recipients while
teachers were in control of the tempo and content. The focus was on
teaching instead of learning. There was a lack of curiosity, authenticity, and the sense-making opportunities that I always craved but
could not articulate.

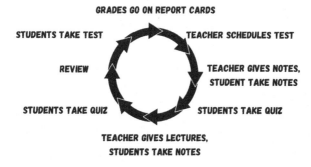

At that time, instructional units generally proceeded like this. The teacher introduced a new topic and new vocabulary. Outside of class, students used a variety of worksheets and flashcards to memorize definitions in preparation for the quiz. Meanwhile, the teacher used text-dense slide presentations to move the entire class through the more complex material. Warm-ups and checks for understanding were used to formatively assess whether the class understood as students' heads bobbed up to the board and down to their handwritten notes. Students who write faster than others had time to chat and check their phones while waiting for the rest of the class to catch up. Other students struggled to keep pace and might have wished they had the time or the courage to ask questions. Then the teacher gave a vocabulary quiz, usually matching or other recall activity. Kids handed-in their work and waited for their peers to finish. At this point, the teacher would assign some type of knowledge deepening assignment, and there would be a review for the next quiz. Kids got the grades on their vocabulary quiz sometime before the big unit test.

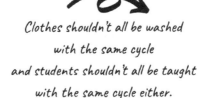

*Clothes shouldn't all be washed
with the same cycle
and students shouldn't all be taught
with the same cycle either.*

Often a great idea for a project or experiment would be discarded because it did not fit into the routine due to the amount of time it would take, the difficulty of reporting the grade, or evaluating student learning. Sometimes teachers who were eager to offer more engaging experiences to students did not feel supported by their administration to take risks. Deviating from the beaten path is frightening and the possibility of failure is real, and without training and guidance, it is not surprising that teachers chose the safest route.

If that is the system, then the system is broken. Many educators feel the same, but what can one teacher do? Very simply stated: any teacher has the power to change the climate of their own classroom. You have the power to change the climate in your classroom.

*YOU have the power
to change the climate in
YOUR classroom*

I've always been told that every great adventure starts with the decision to try. This was why I decided to take the first step toward pursuing my teaching credential. This was quite frightening to me, but this fear was nothing new.

## A Little Backstory

I have held many positions in various occupations. At one time, I was quite comfortable being an office manager and thought that position was the one from which I would retire. My inner child with unquenchable curiosity convinced me to leave the safety of this position to pursue my interest in science and return to college and get my degree in Biology with the goal of working in the field of cancer research. I was married with two young boys. I wanted to model for my sons the importance of having the confidence to pursue your interests and live up to your full potential. I began attending classes full-time while working full-time as well. My employer was gracious in letting me work late nights to accommodate the day labs and classes.

My family — biological and extended — put their full strength behind me, and after four years I had my bachelor's degree in Biology. Upon completing my degree, I worked in a lab, exactly as I had wanted, but it was not what I expected. This disappointment was what led me to my career counselor who recommended I explore a career in education.

So there I was with a freshly printed, new degree, still not fulfilled with my accomplishment. There was a lingering void, some portion of myself left unsatisfied. I returned to the school where I completed my Biology degree to begin taking education courses. For three years, I worked as an instructional assistant during the day and took my education courses at night where I was usually the oldest person in the class. I found that I was also the person who could empathize more readily with nearly everyone I encountered. My meandering path through several different types of jobs and lifetime of experience, richer than what any classroom activity could provide, had given me the ability to see from different viewpoints. My passion for teaching and learning deepened with every course. I constantly wondered how to reach every single student every single day.

The fresh perspective that my college counselor saw in me is what gave me the courage to do things my own way, to see things from the aspect of a learner, and to value the process of learning.

\* \* \*

In the chapters of this book, you will read about my insights, how I addressed them, what I have learned from my experience. I have chosen to incorporate one of my favorite pastimes, hiking, as an analogy to my professional journey. There are many similarities between the training and goal-setting in hiking and those of teaching. Reflecting on hiking experiences encourages me to work toward more challenging terrain or longer distances. Reflecting on teaching encourages me to work toward creating immersive and authentic experiences that fuel curiosity and creating student-centered learning spaces. Each chapter ends with a *Tools For Your Backpack* section with questions, action steps, and suggestions to go deeper into the chapter concepts.

> ***"Talent wins games, but teamwork and intelligence wins championships."***
> ***Michael Jordan***

I hope that you will be able to connect with some aspect of my story so that we, as a community, can use our reflections and connections to learn and share. Let's all learn from our accidental victories and be awesome on purpose.

## Tools For Your Backpack

### Questions

What was the reason that you became a teacher?
Are you being loyal to your intentions?

### Actions

Describe your ideal classroom routine; identify daily, weekly, and monthly routines. Reflect on points where students have rushed ahead or fall behind.

### Go Deeper

Write a vision statement or 50 word summary of what you want your classroom to look and feel like five years from now.

# 2

# THE JOURNEY BEGINS

**We would prepare for a hike by researching, or at least being aware of, the trail ratings.** All the preparation, proper clothing, and equipment can't prepare us for the unexpected so we rely on prior experience to teach us what to bring in our backpacks. But what if this is your first time?

↠ Let's take that first step ↞

## First Step: Me, As A New Teacher

E quipped with my love of science and passion to reach every single student every single day, I accepted a position as a full-time high school biology teacher. Quickly I realized that this is, indeed, where I belong. Sharing my knowledge of science and enthusiasm for learning did not feel like working at all; going to school in the morning was my distinct pleasure. Joyfully, I filled my days with slide presentations, videos, posters, construction paper, markers, and glue, and my nights with grading, researching, and planning. I eagerly devoured any and all professional development opportunities which I used to inform my practice. All of this resulted in more lab activities, projects, and new methods of sharing information about science.

My prior teaching experience with my sister, Winnie, Barbie, and Tiffany paled in comparison to the satisfaction of a room full of human students. A Mark Twain quote lingered in the back of my mind, "The two most important days of your life are the day you were born and the day you find out why."

*"The two most important days of your life are the day you were born and the day you find out why."*

*Mark Twain*

At the end of each day, I sat and thought about my day. I did not plan for this time to be a meaningful reflection. As I simply sat, utterly spent from giving all of myself to my students with my head resting atop my crossed arms on my desk, my thoughts naturally trailed off to what happened during the day. First, my mind wandered to the things that did not go as planned and as a new teacher there were lots of them!

I noticed the rough patches and places where students fell through the cracks.

➤ New vocabulary may not be new to everyone and maybe too complex for others.

➤ Taking handwritten notes does not work for students who think in images or prefer other representations.

➤ Kids who did not do homework were asked to stay for extra help after school or some other punitive action.

➤ Dipsticking gauges the whole class progress but individual students struggle with the pace.

➤ Students who do not know the vocabulary may not understand many of the concepts.

Once I acknowledged the bumps and cracks, I realized that there were just as many — if not more times — when everyone stayed on track. There were even days when we all worked as a team and exceeded my goals. The more days I spent sitting exhausted wondering what I could have done differently, I found I should have been doing more of the things that built a strong team. So I began to look for patterns.

*We do not learn from experience...*

*We learn from reflecting on experience.*

*John Dewey*

While taking my education classes, I underestimated this line by John Dewey, "We do not learn from experience... we learn from reflecting on experience." Daily reflection was the first practice that I decided that I must continue to do with purpose. I reserved 15 minutes at the end of each day to sit quietly and reflect on my own effectiveness, student engagement, and enjoyment. This became such an essential part of my practice that I created a template that I continue to use daily. https://bit.ly/30b0y5P

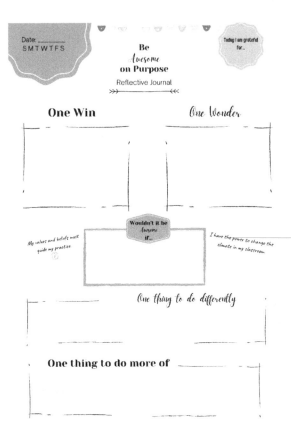

During these reflections I found:

➺ Students work best when they aren't being formally evaluated.
➺ I teach best to small groups.
➺ Students learn best in small groups.
➺ Students learn best when they are engaged.
➺ Student engagement increases with ownership.
➺ Every student is doing the best they can right now.
➺ Every student can do better with time and support.

Just as a hiker uses a map or trail guide, these reflections gave me direction and they continue to be my guide for future planning. The following chapters recount my travels from the base of the most imposing ascents to the astounding views atop their crests. This is my journey to keep the promise made to my 12-year-old self who struggled in junior high: to support each and every student, every single day along their own educational journeys, and to honor my history by committing to never leave a student behind.

## Every Single Student, Every Single Day

Those first few years reminded me that the biggest reward comes from the most challenging journey. While there are times when I have chosen the easy route, the most satisfaction comes from blazing new trails with students as we make meaning of experiences together as we go.

## Tools For Your Backpack

### Questions

What changes can you make to ensure that you are reaching every single student every single day?

Where are the cracks in your instruction? What changes can you make to bridge the cracks so that students don't fall through?

### Actions

Commit part of your day to reflection. Choose a time of day that you are productive and stick with it! It only takes 15 minutes.

Try my Reflective Journal Template https://bit.ly/3ob0y5P

### Go Deeper

Make your actions public, write a blog. Read some inspiring blogs, start here:

Joy Kirr's LiveBinder http://bit.ly/3qw3336

Starr Sackstein https://www.mssackstein.com/blog-1

Human Restoration Project https://www.humanrestorationproject.org/

# 3

# KIDS WORK BEST WHEN THEY ARE NOT BEING FORMALLY EVALUATED

**Hiking trails are rated from easy to extremely difficult.** Ratings
are based on obstructions, steepness of the slope, and distance and
are calculated using a formula that considers elevation gain and
miles.
⇥ Let's go higher and farther together ⇤

I have learned through conversations with teachers from various
grade levels that the insights from my reflections are not limited
to high school teachers. The pressures of curricular timelines and
standardized testing reach down into the elementary grades, too. We
have become so preoccupied with achievement that some of our
practices have been squashing curiosity in the interest of standard-
ization and progress.

In his book *Drive*, Daniel Pink (2009) explains that allowing
people autonomy with clear goals increases intrinsic motivation. As
children, we often experienced intrinsic motivation, the feeling of
satisfaction that causes us to work more intently, more often than we

typically do as adults. Remember the perfect sandcastle after the waves have pommelled multiple attempts, the days-long intricate Lego ® construction project, or the mightiest blanket fortress for your sleepover? Older kids participate in sports where they come to practice and weekend games for either team or individual sports; the reward is not only the completion of the task or competition but the joy of working and the satisfaction of reaching a goal. As adults, we set goals for ourselves. For me, it is running a 10k race.

Putting on those sneakers and heading out the door to run every day is not easy; it is the feeling that I have once the run is done that gets me motivated to do it and to keep on doing it. I want to engage students in a way that causes them to want to do the work because they know the feeling of success that will result.

### Going Higher: Student Agency

There were two small things that frustrated me in the course of a teaching day. One thing is when my high school students raise their hands asking permission to go to the bathroom. Haven't we all experienced this during a lesson? Just when I felt as though all of the students in the class are engaged — not just compliant, actually engaged, participating, and listening — a hand goes up. In that instant, my hopes inflate imagining the questions or observations that a student will share. This could be the conversation that starts a knowledge-deepening investigation. But alas, "Can I go to the bathroom?" Argh, disappointment, of course, a kid can go to the bathroom, but why now when I thought we had something good going?

I started a bathroom sign-out sheet hoping to decrease distractions and stop the loss of momentum when students ask if they can go to the bathroom. The sheet was a way for students to leave the room without having to ask permission. The rules were simple:

- If a student is out, you cannot go; you can only go if no one else is out.
- You must sign out with the time and remember to sign in when you return.

This way I would have a record of who is in the room for accountability and students could go to the bathroom without interrupting the class. It also provided students with some responsibility and use of judgment to determine the best time to leave the room. Teachers are encouraged to be vigilant, uncover naughtiness before it becomes an issue, so I decided to purposefully use this sign-out sheet as a log for myself to look for patterns — to see if students were leaving at the same time every day or in a particular order. What I exposed was not any potential mischief; I found that students were spending less time in the bathroom, probably because they had to sign back in and they knew someone was waiting. I also discovered that students were leaving while I was talking, but rarely when they were working.

This was disheartening. Students were leaving when I was talking; they were missing direct instruction that later would need to be made up. This meant I would have to catch them up or they would feel behind or would ask a friend and they'd both get behind.

My second step was to add a third rule:

- You cannot leave when I am talking or when direct instruction is happening.

With this new rule, I found that students didn't *need* to go to the bathroom; almost no one signed out. Sounds like a win at first. Students are staying in the room and getting the instructional time that I wanted. But after some deep reflection, I realized something different was behind the decrease in bathroom sign-outs.

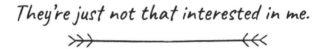

*They're just not that interested in me.*

They were bored listening to me talk; going to the bathroom was probably an escape. This was not easy for me to swallow, but it was a useful piece of information. Now I needed to do something with it.

I decided that I had two options; incentivize staying in the room or give students what they wanted — less talk and more activities — and hope that we all get what we want — more engaged students.

I shortened my direct instruction time. My goal was no more than 25% of class time would be direct instruction. It was received very well, but I was afraid students wouldn't get the information they needed if I wasn't giving it to them.

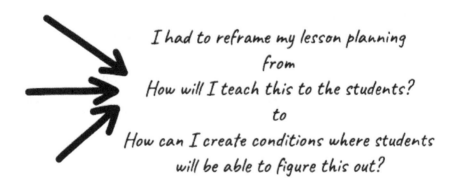

*I had to reframe my lesson planning from How will I teach this to the students? to How can I create conditions where students will be able to figure this out?*

I used station rotations to reinforce and supplement shorter note-taking sessions. Each of the stations required students to employ a different modality to obtain or think more deeply about the notes they had taken. A typical station lab would have six activities:

**Reading:** Differentiated articles and research papers with question sets.

**Modeling:** Inexpensive, easy to construct models that provide a visual representation of the content or concept.

**Active experiences:** Scavenger hunts and kinesthetic activities.

**Drawing/labeling:** Pictorial representations of content or concept; these could be premade and student-created comic strips, labeling, sketchnotes.

**Writing/Reflecting:** Reflection questions including: What is one thing that surprised you? What might someone misunderstand about this topic? How would you help them better understand?

**Explanation Station:** Explain your process as you moved through the stations. Which was the most challenging, why? What skills and knowledge did you use to overcome those challenges?

Reviewing their responses to the explanation station taught me a lot about my students. They explained that sometimes the most challenging part was thinking in a different way — even when they understood the content. This brought me back to my purpose of the assignment; sometimes it is appropriate to assess student understanding of a concept; other times I want to challenge them to think in new ways. These station activities were not an appropriate tool to summatively assess student understanding of a concept. The station activities provided an opportunity for kids to think in new ways and make new connections to content material, and I determined that their best use was as a formative assessment of content and to encourage kids to practice new skills.

I began providing students with choices between assessment options to demonstrate their learning. Choices typically included things such as taking a traditional test, doing a project, creating a presentation, or performing a lab activity. It amazed me that students usually chose the traditional test. Although it was the thing they claimed to like the least, it was the option that was most familiar to them at the time. Even if kids didn't like it, they knew how to prepare and knew what to expect. They were not willing to take risks with new things until they first had the experience of success, like that perfect sandcastle, blanket fort, game day, daily run feeling.

Students had difficulty choosing when given complete autonomy; they needed coaching. I should have started by getting to know my students and providing limited choices designed for students to be able to explore their talents and become comfortable with being agents of their own learning experiences. This would have built a solid foundation upon which I would have been able to construct differentiated tasks that would have been meaningful to every student.

Using this insight, and knowing that challenging work that is delivered in a meaningful context increases student performance (McTighe & Seif, 2011) and intrinsic motivation (Pink, 2009), I worked on a method to gather information about each student's interests and history. The next year, during the first week of school, I provided students with time to complete a "Tell Me About Yourself" survey https://bit.ly/3fIqWRp. Prompts in the survey were designed to elucidate student preferences for learning without asking them directly. Answers to the following prompts have proven very useful to my practice:

> I sleep _____ hours every night.
> _____ makes me happy.
> Knowing the end of a story helps me to focus on reading.
> One thing I wish teachers knew about me is
> Three words that describe me are:

Because I use music, videos, and lots of movement, I include items that will help me provide a comfortable atmosphere for each student in our classroom.

> My favorite kind of music is...
> I feel stressed when _____.
> I work best when _____.

What I learn about each student's interests from these prompts is used to create choice boards for the first curriculum unit of the school year.

> My favorite subject in school is...
> I am taking this class because...
> What I hope to learn from this class is....
> One problem I would like to solve is ...

Providing students with choices for how they communicate their learning is one of the simpler ways that I have found to increase student agency. Choice boards at the beginning of the year typically give students a choice between four options to demonstrate their knowledge of a topic.

I make sure to include options for students who:

- prefer reading
- prefer watching videos
- like to write
- would rather demonstrate their learning using technology.

There is one thing that every student must do; this is in the middle box. There are several options here to demonstrate knowledge and everyone is evaluated by the same rubric. The limited and targeted choices increase student success because they can effectively demonstrate their content knowledge while having the option to explore things outside of their comfort zones. As they try new methods in this safe space, they become more aware of their learning preferences and are willing to take risks.

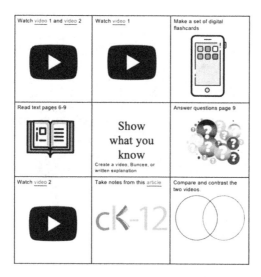

Characteristics of Life Summative Assessment Choice Board.
Choose 2 options that give you a tic-tac-toe
**(the middle box must be included and completed last).**

In addition to empowering students to choose how they demonstrate their learning, I want to give them choices about what they are learning. For this, I began using The Question Formulation Technique (QFT) protocols from Right Question Institute https://rightquestion.org/education/resources/#get-started. This protocol uses a question focus, which could be a prompt, image, or short video, which students use to develop their own questions based on their curiosity and wonderings about the question focus. Using the student questions, I create a set of activities similar to a trail of breadcrumbs for students to follow. Access the complete set of slides for the guided activity here http://bit.ly/AwesomeQFT.

The benefits of QFT are multiple. Ownership of the learning is transferred to students — they own their learning and they know it. I am able to give immediate feedback, and can formatively assess nearly every student in a single class period. While students investigate their interests, I am free to move around the classroom discussing personal motivations and providing individual guidance to students.

> Most recently, I decided to decrease my direct instruction time to 10%. This was a huge task. I had to redesign every aspect of my class. I thought it would be difficult for students to get the information they needed to be successful but I was wrong.
> More about that later

## Going Farther: New Grading Policy

The second small thing that frustrated me was when students asked how to get a higher grade.

*Can I have extra credit?*

*How can I get my grade up?*

When students ask these types of questions, it is because they are not as engaged as I thought they were. When students ask how they can improve their grade, it shows a disconnect between what I am doing and what they are understanding. I wanted to shift this mindset from asking for extra credit to asking, "I do not understand this right now, what can I do?"

At the beginning of the school year, I use traditional knowledge acquisition methods such as notes and research while the options for demonstration of knowledge increase as students become comfortable with this autonomy. There were several small steps over the course of two years that allowed me to do this:

- ❧ Gave my desk away
- ❧ Started walking around the classroom (an average of three miles per day!)
- ❧ Began taking notes, reflections at the end of each class
- ❧ Noticing students' individual preferences for learning
- ❧ Having informative conversations with individual students

I began traveling around the class with the purpose of checking in with students about their work and progress. Feedback became descriptive conversations with individual students: asking them to explain their work, supporting them toward the correct path of thinking. Rather than simply correcting responses, we talked about reasoning, why it would be important to know what they are learning, and how a person might use this knowledge in real life. There was no punishment for wrong answers, just conversations about the thinking that got them there. Students began embracing learning as a process of getting things wrong until eventually, they made fewer mistakes.

Students were learning more deeply and finding ways to apply their learning in ways that were meaningful to them personally. Sparks of ingenuity were flying in the atmosphere in my classes, but my traditional grading practices actually punished students who attempted new, challenging options over the customary, safe ones.

This got me thinking about the types of work that I assigned to students and how I evaluated it. There is a multitude of valuable noncognitive skills that are essential to completing cognitive tasks; not every assignment is a demonstration of learning.

When work is meaningful and everything has a purpose, then there should be some assessment attached; that doesn't mean it is an assessment of student learning. It could be an assessment of my delivery, student engagement, student knowledge or learning, collaboration, ability to follow instructions.

If when I gave assessments it was to determine whether or not students had learned what I was teaching them, then at some level, that was actually an assessment of my effectiveness. It became clear to me that because I am evaluating my own performance, I needed to use these as formative assessments. Just as the station activities, these are no longer included in a student's grade. I began taking the terms evaluate and assess more literally and using them purposefully.

*Not every assignment needs to be evaluated.*

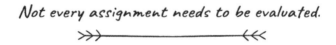

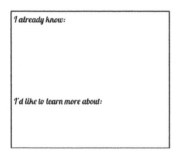

I began intentionally creating assignments that had the purpose of assessing different aspects of student learning and of my teaching. These were as simple as exit slips that determined if students had met the lesson objective for the day and warm-ups to see if kids could recall what they had learned in the previous lesson and are prepared for the next step.

They could also be more complex to see if kids were able to apply their knowledge in meaningful ways while enabling me to identify misconceptions and misunderstandings.

There were also activities designed to reveal general impressions of their disposition. These were ways for me to gather information about factors that might have inhibited their learning including disinterest in the activity or the level of difficulty being a barrier to their learning.

*What is something that a person might not understand about this topic?*



*How would you help them understand it?*

Often, students equate favorite to easiest and most challenging to least favorite. I wanted to encourage the mindset that difficult things can be enjoyable.

*The easiest part about learning [topic] has been:*


*The most challenging part was:*



*My favorite part was:*


*My least favorite was:*

These are as much an assessment of my effectiveness as of students' knowledge. Even if there was only one student in the class that couldn't meet the goal for the day, that is on me. I had made a promise to reach every single student; no one falls through the cracks. These formative assessments became my compass, and I planned my lessons informed by each student's performance. This is not to say that I individualized instruction to each student daily, but I did find a way to create strategic groupings based on whether a student's current performance met expectations or not.

Sometimes groupings facilitated students supporting one another.

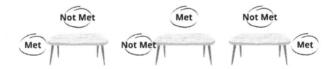

A student who has met performance expectations is paired with a student who has not yet. Both students benefit from the pairing; the student who has met the PE reinforces their learning by helping the student who has not and the student who has not has the benefit of a new perspective of the content.

Other times, groupings enabled me to focus on students in need of extra support while other students worked on enrichment activities.

I began seeing assessment through a new lens; this led to my next cascade of questions.

- ➤ If an assignment is designed to be an assessment of my effectiveness, then how can I use that to also assess student learning?
- ➤ If a student performs poorly on that assignment, then isn't that my fault and not theirs? Could that be true of any assignment?
- ➤ My job is to teach children; if they are not learning, then whose fault is that?
- ➤ Should grades reflect student participation and my effectiveness?

After a good, hard look, I had to admit that my grade book did not accurately reflect what students know and are able to do because student participation and my effectiveness did impact grades. Knowing this, I set out to change my grading policies, the way my assignments are written, and the way they are delivered.

*"Grades are not compensation.*
*Grades are communication."*
*Rick Wormeli*

My goals for students were clearly articulated for each class, lesson, and unit. I have always posted the daily goals; the language used is meant to be accessible to all students. Goals are written in the form of "Today you will be able to..." with statements that do not reveal specific processes so that students have the freedom to decide how they will demonstrate their learning.

*Today you will be able to apply your knowledge of cell theory to clarify an example of evolution.*

*Today you will be able to use words or images to explain the difference between heterozygous and homozygous.*

To encourage students to personalize these goals, I began assigning student blogs to increase reflection and metacognition. When I asked students to blog about their goals and progress, many students would write about the grade they wanted to have at the end of the term. Some were able to explain how they would achieve that grade. Sometimes they would explain the reason for their grade was to be on the honor roll or maintain a GPA or for athletic eligibility. As I read through these, I was shocked at a couple of things. First, the grade was a shallow goal; when I pressed the student to explain what is an A or B they could not explain it to me, not even 11th and 12th-grade students! They explained that they could get this grade by doing homework and studying for tests. Clearly, these students would need some support if they were going to set meaningful goals.

Eventually, goals began to change — the process and reason for them changed also. Students were finding meaningful reasons to participate in class. It was no longer about the honor roll; it was about the satisfaction of knowing something that they did not know before, being able to transfer their knowledge, actually use it, and teach other people. Some goals were to learn new things or simply try something new. Like sandcastles and blanket forts, the satisfaction of accomplishment was its own reward.

## Tools For Your Backpack

### Questions

What percent of class time is direct instruction?

How can you lead a class without standing in front of them?

What can you do to get to know students' interests early in the school year?

### Actions

Give ownership of one of your daily practices to your students.

Identify an available tool that can help you deliver content and assessments at the same time to all of your students while they move at their own pace.

Switch an interim assessment to an opportunity to provide targeted, descriptive, actionable feedback to students.

### Go Deeper

Do some quick research into choice boards and learning menus.

A.J. Juliani updates these resources regularly

http://ajjuliani.com/the-ultimate-guide-to-choice-boards-and-learning-menus/

# 4

# I TEACH BEST WITH SMALL GROUPS

**As the trails that we choose to hike become more difficult, we prepare ourselves by researching** the terrain and the obstacles that we can expect to encounter. The easiest trails are paved; the most difficult, double black diamond trails, have loose and falling rocks, uneven terrain, and exposure to drops.

↝ Here is how I navigated my first black diamond trail ↜

When I started the transformation of my classroom policies and routines, I intended to foster an environment where students could be more independent and more engaged. What happened was surprising and enlightening; students began rushing to get to our class, they were not asking to leave, they were not signing out, they knew what their goals were, they knew the learning target, and they were empowered to reach those goals and targets. They were given the necessary tools and supports and they were off! Now, I had the time to support students in ways that were actually helpful to them without feeling rushed. Some students needed more support than others; the difference was that I was not rushed, the students were not rushed, and everyone still met their targets.

Most teachers that I have spoken with agree that they teach better to small groups, yet our class sizes sometimes prohibit a teaching environment that works best for everyone. In my experience, the only advantage of large class sizes is that, because they do not ordinarily allow for support to small groups of students or to students individually, at the college-level, large classes make students responsible for their learning. My goal has been to make the best of the opportunity in front of me by encouraging and maintaining student autonomy while creating a culture of support and empowering each student to seek knowledge that will be of meaning to them personally.

### The First Obstacle: Class Size

My class sizes were not going to get any smaller; I needed to organize my classes and units of instruction so that kids can work in small groups more often. After considering several options and observing a variety of different classrooms, problem-based learning seemed as though it would be a move toward a solution.

I began a hybrid model of problem-based learning, using short-term projects during which I could assess each student's ability to

- follow instructions,
- take the lead role in a group,
- work effectively in a group, and
- work independently

all while they were demonstrating their content knowledge. Students immediately bought-in to the authenticity of projects such as solving drainage problems for houses along the local river, reducing the number of invasive species in our nature sanctuary, and debating the use of 3D printed tissues.

I was participating in a *What School Could Be* book study around the same time that I was exploring these new types of projects. The discussions helped me to synthesize some of my thoughts about the importance of engagement, facilitating a student-led classroom, and the impact these shifts would have on overall student achievement and enjoyment.

In the book, Ted Dintersmith (2018) traveled around the country visiting schools hoping to identify what practices were most effective for student learning. He determined that classroom environments where students were the most engaged provide the following ingredients: purpose, essentials, agency, knowledge. I strongly recommend reading his book, preferably with a group of colleagues, community members, and school leaders. As a result of this book study, I was determined to cultivate an environment that provided students with C.A.R.E.

**C**HOICES ABOUT WHAT AND HOW THEY LEARN.

**A**UTHENTIC EXPERIENCES THAT ARE MEANINGFUL TO THEM INDIVIDUALLY.

**R**EAL-WORLD APPLICATIONS FOR THEIR LEARNING.

**E**MPOWERMENT TO SHARE THEIR LEARNING OUTSIDE OF THE CLASSROOM.

I already had a routine that provided students with choices for knowledge demonstration. Choice boards, descriptive feedback conversations, strategic group work, and reflective exit slips were not just helping students develop an understanding of how they can best show their learning, they were also increasing intrinsic motivation! I decided to increase the number of options that I offered students for knowledge acquisition as a way to capitalize on this accidental discovery.

**Rough Terrain: Decreasing Direct Instruction**

The decrease in my direct instruction time started with a method I called "notes two ways." The Google Slides notes that would ordinarily be given in class through lectures were posted in Google Classroom and students decided if they wanted to follow along with me at the front of the class near the board or move at their own pace at the back of the class. (It is worth noting here that the front of my class is quite cozy, with alternative seating including a modular sofa, pillows, and a large round table.)

Initially, most students decided to sit up front and take notes at my pace; they stopped and asked questions just as a typical lecture would proceed. Students who chose the self-paced option sat quietly in the back writing their notes and asking questions when they had them. I walked around the room answering questions and advancing slides, checking progress, and understanding. This method replaced the typical note-taking classes that usually occurred once per week. Over time, students started moving toward the back of the room, deciding they would rather move at their own pace knowing they can still ask questions when they have them.

If it sounds a little chaotic that's because it was! It was the best option I had at the time, but I knew I needed to make changes. So I decided to ask the kids for feedback. I created a Google Form that asked questions about classroom procedures and how they felt about our new note-taking process.

Prompts included:

When I come to class I feel _____.

My favorite thing about this class is _____.

My least favorite thing about this class is _____.

Class would work better for me if _____.

Student feedback told me that they liked the idea of moving at their own pace while having me available to answer their questions but there was too much going on at the same time. I did not disagree. I wanted to be with the students who were working independently and take time to walk among those students while addressing the students in the front, but I could not be in two places at the same time. It just wasn't right yet. Again, my mistake was offering students too many choices while providing limited guidance.

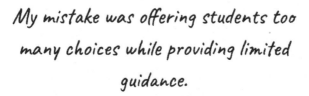

*My mistake was offering students too many choices while providing limited guidance.*

I wanted students to be able to move at their own pace while getting the support they needed from me and ensuring they were getting the content that was being delivered to them. My solution was to eliminate the teacher-paced option and embed checkpoints into the slides. In hindsight, this seems risky, but it made sense and still does.

Checkpoints were quick prompts such as:

- Write 3 wonderings
- What might a person misunderstand about this topic
- Construct a model
- Because, But, So
- Quick write / quick draw
- Sketchnotes
- 3-2-1

**Write 3 Wonderings**

This is used to capture what students are thinking as they are introduced to a topic. The prompt is, "What are you wondering right now?" followed by nudges for kids to fill in, "I wonder why..." "I wonder if..." "I wonder how..." "I wonder when...".

Get a copy here http://bit.ly/AwesomeWonders.

# WRITE 3 WONDERINGS

### WHAT ARE YOU WONDERING RIGHT NOW?

I WONDER WHY...

I WONDER IF...

I WONDER HOW...

I WONDER WHEN...

## What Might a Person Misunderstand About This Topic

This activity allows students to explain a misunderstanding without feeling insecure. I use this prompt in the middle of a lesson sequence. Students are free to explain what someone might misunderstand about the topic they are currently working on without the fear of judgment.

## Construct a Model

There are times when a concept can be visualized as a three-dimensional model. I find it incredibly insightful when kids construct models of things such as processes and physical objects that they are learning about. This gives us the opportunity to talk through complicated topics together and empowers students to express their understanding in a different way.

## Quick Write / Quick Draw and Sketchnotes

At any time in a learning sequence, asking students to jot, doodle, or sketch their ideas has been a great way for me to determine the next steps in my planning. Giving students the freedom to show their understanding in ways other than words helps validate their learning process and gives me a peek into their thought process.

## Because, But So

This is a student favorite! I provide a prompt and students respond in three sentences beginning with because, but, and so. Here is an example.

Learning is fun.

*Because* we get to use models.

*But* it is also hard work.

*So* we try our hardest every day.

This is especially true when students work in pairs or groups of three to hand-off to another student. The answers to this prompt reveal students' depth of understanding.

Get a copy here http://bit.ly/AwesomeBBB.

Because, But, So

**Respond to this statement**

" _____ "

Because...

But...

So...

**3-2-1**

I use this at the end of a class period or learning sequence. The prompts are "Summarize 3 things you learned today," "What are 2 things that surprised you today?" and "What is 1 question that you have about what you learned today?"

Get a copy here http://bit.ly/Awesome3-2-1.

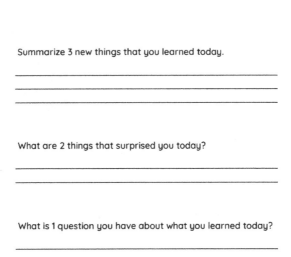

## 3-2-1 Checkpoint

Summarize 3 new things that you learned today.

_____

_____

_____

What are 2 things that surprised you today?

_____

_____

What is 1 question you have about what you learned today?

_____

These checkpoints increased in complexity as the notes progressed and it worked really well. I naturally spent more time with students who needed support or encouragement and I could readily observe whether or not students understood what they were learning. Students could also see what their peers were doing and ask one another for help as they progressed through the notes.

I had accidentally initiated visible thinking and learning. Only after watching student interactions after a couple of days did I notice that students were learning from one another, openly sharing ideas and understandings. I recalled from a previous graduate class there were extensive studies on evidence-based practices based on visible thinking and learning. The work of Ritchhart, Church, and Morrison and of Project Zero out of Harvard University http://www.pz.harvard.edu/ has been incredibly helpful for me to build-up my student-centered learning environment. Using tasks and prompts intentionally can shine a light on the learning process of each student. This illuminates thinking pathways — not just for me — but for students as well. By asking questions in the right way, I began to elicit responses that displayed student misconceptions early in the learning process. In my classroom, these types of activities are ungraded; students confidently try their best with no fear of failure or damage to their grade. Learning became a process where mistakes are visible and shared openly to help others improve their understanding.

This visible learning added a new, unexpected level of engagement. Students were encouraged to look at what their classmates were doing and to ask and answer questions. For some, this is a big shift from the traditional classroom experience where students are discouraged from looking at each other's work. Learning evolved into an open, collaborative process where sharing and learning from one another is valued and expected. But they had to put things into their own words and be prepared to explain their work. As I circulated among students while they worked on gathering knowledge and sharing ideas, I asked questions such as

"What do you see here?"

"What prior knowledge can you connect this to?"

"What do you wonder?"

"How might someone use this knowledge?"

I invited students to join in the conversation, asking them to share their insights with one another. The connections between content and real-life became more clear to students and their engagement deepened.

Student-paced notes were a way to scaffold autonomy to build their capacity to work in a student-centered class, but they were still just notes. I needed a way to help kids to understand and be invested in the learning goal. I began exploring methods of content delivery that would cultivate C.A.R.E.

*It was time to empower students to choose not just what they learned but how they learned it.*

Hyperdocs was an option. These are documents with step-by-step instructions and links for students to access rich content such as videos, interactives, and activities. These give students the freedom to work through lessons at their own pace. Purposefully adding in checkpoints with reflective questions makes these a powerful learning tool. Creating them and reordering the items and inserting interactive content was time-consuming for me with disproportionate returns for the kids. Then I discovered Wakelet. https://learn.wakelet.com/. Wakelet is a platform where multiple types of content can be added, reordered, and delivered to multiple audiences in different ways. It allows for different types of publishing that permits viewers to contribute, copy, or share depending on the permissions set by the owner. Currently, this platform is ideal for what I am trying to accomplish.

The ultimate differentiation was an unintended result.

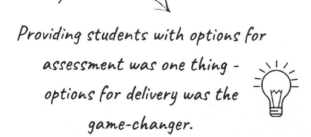

*Providing students with options for assessment was one thing - options for delivery was the game-changer.*

## Obstacles: Imprecise Grades

As my routine for station rotations and visual learning began to evolve, the need to rethink my grading practices became clear. Watching students experience the productive struggle of learning to set goals was our new classroom ecosystem and this required a contemporary grading system.

I became convinced that content knowledge is the only thing that should be assessed formally, not to discount the other skills students acquire and require to be successful. Skills including communication, collaboration, and listening as well as qualities such as empathy are explicitly taught through many activities, but I feel as though these should not be included in a student's grade. These should be reported through descriptive feedback and discussions with students and their families whenever possible. Realizing this, I needed to develop a system to informally assess and report progress on student soft skills separate from their content knowledge and learning.

Initially, I set up my grade book with new categories. Where traditionally there would be homework, participation, quiz, test, I used the categories formative assessment, quiz, project. The grading software that my school used allowed me to set up formative assessments to be weighted as 0% of the final grade. Any soft skills were reported in the form of comments on the report card and messages to home (positive and negative).

*Just 2 Gradebook Categories*

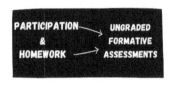

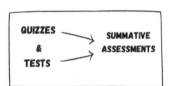

Anything completed outside of class, with a group, or with some other support that did not provide direct evidence that the student could perform a task independently comprised the formative assessments category. My reasoning for this was that I could not ensure what a student actually did themselves based on that assignment. For example, a warm-up done in class with a partner, homework, group work. Any of these assignments can be used as an indicator of a skill but not an indicator of what a student independently knows and is able to do; it is very difficult to know exactly how much was done by a particular student.

Perhaps during the warm-up:

- one student did more work than the other;
- or one student understood one concept more clearly than the other student.

There is no practical way for me to determine what work was done by which student in these cases.

In the case of homework:

- Perhaps a student didn't do the homework for any number of reasons: remember everyone is doing the best they can with the tools they have today.

- Perhaps they have a sibling, parent, neighbor, or anyone at home who can help them.
- Perhaps students work together during a study hall or after school: which is fantastic! Collaboration gets things done but it makes determining the skills and knowledge of individual students difficult.
- Maybe, one student did the homework and other students copied that work feeling the pressure to be done, a behavior learned from years of traditional grade culture.

When students work in groups, it is even more difficult to determine who did which portion. Even the most carefully planned groups can be foiled by well-intentioned students who want to help out a friend or an aggressive grade-getter. Group work provides an opportunity for numerous soft skills. I have determined that using group work as an opportunity to observe students purposefully is much more beneficial to me than primarily evaluating their performance of content learning. Through my continued research on grading, something that Robert Marzano said stuck with me: "Grades are so imprecise that they are almost meaningless."

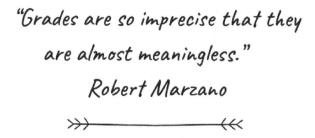

"Grades are so imprecise that they are almost meaningless."
Robert Marzano

I made a big shift here; I stopped assessing homework and classwork and started giving targeted feedback on these assignments. When students submitted work, they were not given a grade immediately; instead, they were given feedback and — not just an oppor-tunity — but the expectation that they will use my feedback to improve their performance. Feedback centered around what was correct, where there were misunderstandings, and how to move forward.

Sometimes, a student wouldn't take advantage of opportunities to improve. When this happened, I investigated what it is about their history, their confidence, or their schedule that kept them from trying again knowing that they could only improve from their first draft. Student buy-in increased and their performance improved. The behavior in my classes was markedly changed; students began asking more questions, admitting when things were tough, helping each other, unashamed and unpressured. This process was time-consuming, and it was sometimes impossible to provide feedback in a timeframe that was sensible without spending long nights and weekends reading and commenting on student work. I needed a more feasible method.

I used Google Forms to automate feedback by attaching videos to responses. These included videos that I made myself and others that I found that addressed misunderstandings elicited by incorrect responses and deepened understanding when students provided correct responses. Once kids were in the habit of navigating this new landscape of experimenting with new learning, using feedback, and reflecting independently, goal-setting became a natural next step. At the launch of a new unit, I provided students with the learning objectives and facilitated conversations with prompts like:

"Why do people need to know this?"
"What can someone do with this knowledge?"
"Where might we learn more about this?"

This series of questions evolved into students setting goals for themselves and creating their own rubrics. Each student decided what their goal for the next unit would be based on what interested them about the learning objectives. We used a sample rubric as a model to determine how they wanted to be evaluated and students wrote their own criteria for success.

66 *Very few things are as dangerous as a bunch of incentive-driven individuals trying to play it safe.* 99
*Alfie Kohn*

It was risky and completely worth it. Students were already familiar with reading the learning objectives and determining where their interests would intersect; releasing the next layer of power to them came naturally. We devoted one class period to 1:1 student conferences to align their interests with learning targets at the beginning of each subsequent learning sequence.

## Tools For Your Backpack

### Questions

How can you begin to engage students in a way that causes them to want to do the work because they know the feeling of success that will result?

What do you do to ensure that the time students spend in your class is valuable?

### Actions

Change one graded assignment to a no-stakes group learning opportunity. Instead of assigning a number grade give descriptive, actionable feedback. Provide students with time to read and address the feedback.

### Go Deeper

Design a no-stakes formative assessment that provides immediate feedback. A gallery walk, ignite talk, Google Form, or Kahoot.

Check out *Differentiated Instruction in the Teaching Profession* by Kristen Koppers

Check out the work of Carol Ann Tomlinson https://differentiationcentral.com/

# 5

# STUDENTS LEARN BEST IN SMALL GROUPS

**Hikers travel in teams because there is safety and support in numbers.** The team is stronger when members contribute varied experiences and unique perspectives.

↝ Building a classroom team ↜

## Safety In Numbers: Building A PLN

S chool, like hiking, is not a race. The goal is for every person to get through to the end safely and with a feeling of accomplishment. Considering this spirit, it makes more sense to encourage students to work as a team to reach goals: to learn and experience new things, to get to graduation, to the trail's end.

The popularity of Edcamps, conferences, and professional learning networks makes it seem as though educators see the importance of collaboration. We are all helping one another through the rough patches to get better as a whole. This is the mindset that we must also inspire in our students.

> "A PLN is a tool that uses social media and technology to collect, communicate, collaborate and create with connected colleagues anywhere at any time. Participating educators, worldwide, make requests and share resources. Each individual educator becomes a potential source of information. Collecting these sources in a location to access them is the PLN. There are no two PLNs that are the same."
> Tom Whitby, How Do I Get a PLN: Edutopia, 2013

Group work can be difficult to manage. When students work in groups, it takes some effort by the teacher to keep track of who is doing what works in order to understand what content is mastered by individual students. Students become frustrated when the group dynamic disallows or does not encourage individual student voices. There always will be a quiet student, an outspoken student, and an expert student. In my experience, when students are not eager to participate in group work, it is because they have little control over the grade they will receive. Teachers can sometimes misinterpret individual student contributions to the group and assign grades that are inaccurate.

This is a point where I begin to diverge from some educators. Instead of reducing the amount of group work because of the difficulty in teasing out individual grades, I rethought how I graded group work.

I already knew that I teach better to small groups; now I know for certain that students learn better in small groups and all students can benefit from the collaborative experience. Because of the changes to my practice, students were beginning to flourish. I was beginning to cultivate CARE through partner work and collaboration to solve problems, but the choices that I was offering to students were not sufficient to increase agency and self-efficacy.

"If you want to go far,

go together;

if you want to go fast,

go alone."
–Unknown

I began incorporating learning menus. Learning menus increase the number of options and work toward self-directed learning. These give students more opportunities to decide how they will demonstrate their learning while still providing some teacher guidance. In BISDWiredTeamBlog, Tommy Spall has phenomenal examples and templates for learning menus that include student instructions for the various technology options. https://brenhamtechdaily.blogspot.com/2017/10/teaching-tip-thursday-digital-menu-for.html

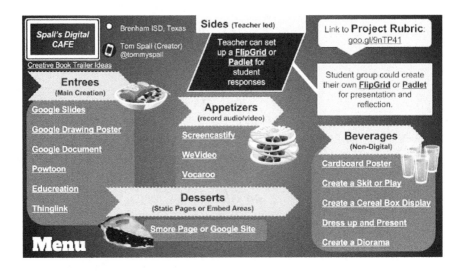

I replaced a couple of traditional units with problem-based learning: projects where students must solve problems using current knowledge but require additional information from peers, experts, or research.

What I found from watching students collaborating in class was that they were eager to offer their expertise or passion for a particular topic. They were familiar with working in small groups during station labs, so the idea of collaboration was not new but having a more open goal was.

### Notes Two Ways 2.0

I revisited the Notes Two Ways routine (described in Chapter 4) looking for ways to increase student independence while providing support when needed. The goal was to empower students to move at their own pace and to identify misunderstandings early. I began embedding different styles of videos into the note slides for students to choose from. These were followed by a short task that I could check and that would initiate some discussion among students. Depending on understanding, I could then initiate whole-class, small group, or individual discussions. If I found that the majority of students had a common misconception, then a group discussion would help to clarify that. If there were students whose work showed that they were meeting or exceeding expectations, then those students could facilitate small group discussions. Other times there may be individual students who need more time; remember students are moving at their own pace and because some students naturally move faster than others, whole group discussions usually only happen at the beginning of a new topic.

This worked very well for me and my students; I could offer small group assistance to all students and 1:1 to many. But notes are still just notes. Technology has improved our ability to communicate with people all over the world in real-time or to collaborate with peers in the classroom down the hall or across the globe. This reminds me of a Henry Ford quote about faster horses.

**66** *If I had asked people what they wanted, they would have said faster horses.* **99**

*Henry Ford*

I find myself using new tools to do the same thing I've always done, just in a different way. There must be a better way, an even more active, engaging, and purposeful way for kids to gather information and demonstrate learning.

Knowledge acquisition evolved from slide presentations to a multisensory experience. I gathered and shared resources that included:

Options for reading:
➺ Stories, excerpts from books
➺ Articles professional journals and news publications
➺ Textbook chapters both digital and physical


Options for listening:
➺ Podcasts
➺ Interviews


Options for watching:
➺ TED talk
➺ Khan Academy


Opensource:
➺ PBS/Discovery Interactives


I shared these with students using choice boards. The learning objectives were displayed clearly for students and they were empowered to determine which of the delivery options worked best for them. The unintended consequence of increased ownership and engagement was the result of these knowledge acquisition choice boards. Students know when they need help and can articulate their needs clearly. This was due to the new classroom discourse where students were active creators of knowledge rather than passive recipients.

Class discussions start with common talking points that I designed from the learning targets; some are linked to previous learning while others stretch students' thinking about new content material. Students collaborate jigsaw-style using resources that I have provided to investigate while they create a product that displays their learning process. Typically, Venn diagrams, t-chart, sketchnotes, flowcharts, or a written summary on a large sheet of paper have been used to visualize thinking. While kids work, I circulate, ask questions, and suggest where they might find answers; rarely do I have to answer questions. Periodically, students stop working and gallery walk. They travel around the room to see the visual displays that other groups have created. Students use post-it notes to add to the display with comments, insights, or questions.

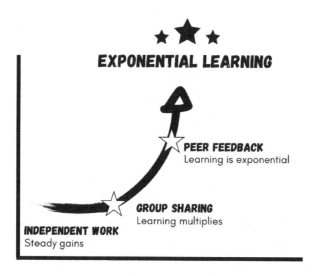

Students were asking better questions and trying to find the answers themselves. They were helping each other — not by giving each other answers but by exploring the answers to questions together. They began to view classmates as resources for learning while developing relationships and taking pride in their accomplishments.

I had accidentally found a way to effectively improve student learning outcomes and engagement. Learning and student self-efficacy increased exponentially when they collaborated and provided feedback to one another.

## Support Of The Team: Putting What I Learned Into Action

I've said in the past that I am in this profession because I love science and I love to teach, and I don't feel comfortable judging the work of others. It is difficult for me to articulate the difference between grading and judgment. This can also reach into judging why students behave the way they do. While there will always be evaluation and assessment in school, it is important for me to deliberately remove any judgment from the process.

For years, I read many books and articles on educational research and leadership. These books were filled with ideas to increase student ownership of their learning and in turn improve learning outcomes. I also looked at what I learned from those books and wondered which strategy or technique I would be able to implement in my practice. The pressures of being a classroom teacher cannot be overstated; state standardized testing milestones, administrative evaluations, students who strive for admission to top colleges and universities, students for any number of reasons who have difficulty participating in class all add up and weigh on the shoulders of teachers. With all of this, adding to my routine seemed undoable, and replacing a current practice could be risky with a disastrous ending.

*My values and beliefs must guide my practice.*

Finally, after years of reflection and experimentation, I am becoming an expert on myself and I know that I have more to learn. I have learned that my values and beliefs must guide my practice. I began to follow these every day in my teaching and personal life. I am an ordinary flawed human being and I do not feel comfortable being the judge of other people. My grading practices reflect these values; students are always given multiple attempts at learning. When a student doesn't take advantage of these multiple attempts, I try to figure out why the student does not take the opportunity. I ask myself what has happened in that student's history that lets them reassign themselves to someone else's judgment of them when the judgment does not match how they feel about themselves or their ability. It may be that they do not think they can do any better and are satisfied with their first attempt — even when I know that they can do better.

## Tools For Your Backpack

### Questions

Do students in your classroom feel like they are on a team?

How can you build team spirit that does not focus on competition?

In what way can you make knowledge acquisition an active process for students?

### Actions

Identify one thing that you are currently doing simply because you have always done it that way.

Change the notes for one of your lessons to a student-centered experience.

### Go Deeper

Explore the work at Harvard Project Zero

http://www.pz.harvard.edu/

# 6

# STUDENTS LEARN BEST WHEN THEY ARE ENGAGED
## ENGAGEMENT INCREASES WITH OWNERSHIP

**Even with research, planning, and partnerships, hiking trips can change unexpectedly.** Perhaps weather or injury can thwart plans — experienced hikers make difficult situations look easy. ⇢ Learning to make changes on the fly ↤

### Changing Weather: Be Prepared To Pivot

Once I have introduced a topic to students, I give them some time to explore. They explore what they already know, they discuss with one another the experiences they have had related to the topic, and they share their ideas with the class. Even after spending time getting to know students at the beginning of the year and through conversations in class, there are still things that surprise me. There are still things that surprise students about themselves. It is rewarding when I discover something or when a class activity helps a student discover something about themselves.

Here are two stories that taught me about how important it is for students to own their learning.

## The Firefighter

My anatomy class for juniors and seniors is filled with students who take the class for a variety of reasons. Some know that they want to pursue careers in a medical field, some want to learn more about their own bodies, and others just need the credit to graduate.

This is the story of a student who changed my outlook on teaching. He was a senior and was not known to be the most devoted student of science — a hard worker well-loved by everyone, the classic under-achiever. The year he was in my class was the first year I decided to try genius hour. I called these passion projects and gave students one hour every week to work on anything they chose. While students were engaged in their projects, the challenge I gave myself was to discover what students were passionate about and incorporate these topics into my regular teaching routine. The heterogeneous mix of students resulted in a range of projects from children's books to prosthetic hands and everything in between. While students investigated their interests, I took notes and made sure to include these in future lessons. These projects blurred the line between knowledge acquisition and demonstration and became a bridge to deeper learning. Students became engaged in their iterative process of learning, responding to feedback, and pursuing extensions specific to their interests. Learning became conversational — authentic two-way dialog that drove their interest and improved their understanding.

This student (the firefighter) decided he wanted to incorporate his work with the local fire department and learn about burns and how they are treated. I watched as this young man devoted his hour of class time plus attending EMT classes at night. He had a true gift for helping people. I suspect that he knew this about himself and never shared it. Possibly he needed some support to realize that it is okay to pursue goals that seemed unexpected. At the end of the semester when students presented their projects to the class, he sat patiently and watched all 24 other students' projects and finally got the nerve to present his at the very end. His face was beaming. He was in the zone as he wore the protective equipment from the fire department as he explained the materials in the suit and demonstrated how to treat different types of burns on the scene using a fellow student as a model. He even went on to explain the treatment that a victim would receive in the emergency room once he had transported them there.

The class erupted in applause as he stood in front of them wearing 60 pounds of fireproof clothing next to the model who he had treated for multiple burn injuries. Students asked questions about why he wanted to do this dangerous job. They were completely engrossed by his passion and compassion for others; they never looked at him the same way again and he was never seen as a classic underachiever ever again. He emerged as a leader that day.

## Students Leading With Empathy

There have been times when I invite the students with severe special needs and their teacher into our classroom. This is always a memorable experience for both groups of students. Students sometimes wonder what it's like to be in the other kids' class while other students don't realize how completely different their experiences are from others even though their paths cross multiple times a day.

**More about "soft skills"**

The term soft skills gives the impression that they are
unimportant.
I prefer to call them non-cognitive skills.
The University of Chicago Consortium on Chicago School
Research has a comprehensive explanation of non-cognitive
skills and their benefits to students.

They identify several behaviors and skills that many would
call soft skills including
Organizational Skills
Tenacity
Self-Discipline
Metacognitive Strategies
Goal-Setting
Empathy
Cooperation

According to their research, these skills can be divided into 5
categories of non-cognitive factors.
Academic Behaviors
Academic Perseverance
Learning Strategies
Social Skills
Academic Mindset

These build upon one another to improve student self-
efficacy and ultimately - academic success.

The first year that we did this, we used an activity that I planned
for my students to help the other class to learn about the nervous
system. The goal for the day was for students to understand that
neurons speak to each other and that signals pass from one to the
other. As my students worked with their guests, some of them reno-
vated this activity. They naturally understood how to help the
visiting students better understand the concept; they created neck-
laces and manipulatives and introduced vocabulary. I watched my
students demonstrate their knowledge of nerve impulses. I was
happy to see that they knew it well enough to teach someone else.
But I also saw students intrinsically motivated to share their
learning and try to help students with different experiences, back-
grounds, and abilities have some common experience by making a
representation of a completely abstract concept more visible and
public.

## Making It Look Easy: Behind The Scenes

Sometimes there are comments in the teachers' lounge; colleagues have sometimes asked me how I "get away with" letting kids have fun all the time and not having traditional lesson plans and giving traditional grades. While I am thankful it is evident that I am enjoying what I do every day, this conversation leads me to believe that they have the misconception that I'm not working .... but I AM. Building relationships through meaningful activities is work and the planning is done behind the scenes. Look into the classroom and you will never see me grading papers or planning lessons; the time I have together with students is spent together with students. While I circulate talking to each student every day, I check-in with them. We talk about science, projects, and life. We share stories that connect us and connect our lives to what they are learning. I provide feedback about what they are working on and encourage them to share their stories with their peers.

The rewards of this work may happen immediately or somewhere down the road. I am confident that motivation, reflection, and empathy are essential to forming a long-term relationship with learning and that knowledge is more permanent when it can be connected to a meaningful experience.

There is tremendous value in group activities for students. Although I feel that it is inequitable to evaluate students' content knowledge, the benefit of collaborative work cannot be ignored. Because of this, I design group work primarily for students to become better collaborators. The specific content work is not difficult; it is the group task that is meant to be the challenge. Recall I provide feedback on soft skills in comments rather than including them in the calculation for the number grade that is reported on student transcripts. I use three basic types of collaborative work.

At the introduction of a topic, students work together in knowledge discovery activities. In the middle of a learning sequence, students work together to reinforce their knowledge and support one another, and at the end of a unit, students work together to share and display their work.

**Knowledge Discovery Activities:**

- Question Focus Technique (described in Chapter 3)
- Standards Deconstruction
- Problem Solvers

**Standards Deconstruction**

Provide students with the learning objectives or content standards. After reading and discussing, have groups determine what they might learn and be able to do as a result of their learning.

**Problem Solvers**

Provide students with the learning objectives or content standards. After reading and discussing, have groups decide what problems someone who understands those concepts might be able to solve.

## Knowledge Reinforcement Activities

- Practical Use Activities
- Jigsaws

### Practical Use Activities

Provide students with problems that can be solved with the new knowledge that they have gained. For example, after learning the differences between male and female skeletons, I have students identify bones in a crime scene and create a story for how they might have gotten there.

### Jigsaws

For this two-part activity, use a challenge with multiple parts or an assortment of articles on the same topic and assign students to complete a section. Next, form new groups with one person from each group from step 1 (who have completed the same task) and have them share what they have learned from their activity. Using this technique enables me to give challenging and lengthy reading selections that I may not otherwise be able to due to time constraints. This is also a fabulous way to differentiate reading by giving the same topic at different Lexile ® levels.

## Knowledge Display Activities

- Fairs
- Campaigns

### Fairs

Student groups create public displays of their learning that we present in the school media center during the school day. Inspired by science fairs, during these activities students celebrate what they have learned by creating activities or games for visitors to play.

### Campaigns

Students choose the favorite thing they learned and devise a campaign to compete with their classmates. This activity is designed based on political campaigns and has students write and deliver speeches, posters, and social media campaigns. The "winner" is determined by a school-wide poll.

### Adjusting To Injury: Dealing With Setbacks

In *The Power of Moments*, Chip Heath explains how taking advantage of the heightened awareness and excitement of unexpected events can make moments memorable and even give them additional meaning.

There are several times in the year when we can predict disruptions to our ordinary daily school routine. They happen predictably every year, yet I had never taken advantage of them. I made a list that included fire drills, picture day, inclement weather delays, and pep rallies and then made a file of plans similar to sub plans for each of them. I intentionally began seeing these as opportunities for authentic learning experiences rather than disruptions.

This might not have been possible if grading was my first concern. Because I have given myself the freedom to use just two grading categories, my focus can be on providing meaningful learning experiences rather than meeting grading deadlines.

> 66 *The most exciting phrase to hear in science,*
> *the one that heralds new discoveries,*
> *is not "Eureka" but "That's funny..."* 99
> *Isaac Asimov*

Take a moment to think of how you might use these disruptions to enrich your curriculum.

- Fire drill: In science, I can easily relate this to fight or flight response and the chemistry of fire extinguishers.
- Picture day: Topics such as the history of photography, aperture, the importance of light, and physiology of vision are some interesting STEM topics. If you want to add something fun, explore Google Arts and Culture's art selfie app https://artsandculture.google.com/camera/selfie.
- Inclement weather delay: Take advantage of students' shared experience to explore various weather phenomena.
- Pep rally: I discuss the importance of community and share amazing examples in nature such as ant colonies and The Mother Tree Project https://mothertreeproject.org/.

**That was unexpected!**

Perhaps it's because of my science background that I am so comfortable with seeing unexpected results and using them to move forward. When things don't go according to plan, it just means there were options that we did not anticipate; sometimes they are better than expected, and sometimes we have to shift our perspective and reframe our thinking. Some of my most effective lessons have been the ones that didn't go as planned. It is okay to just say to yourself,

"That was unexpected," and see it as a learning opportunity.

## Tools For Your Backpack

### Questions

How can you ensure students are learning when they own the learning?
What is a recurring disruption that you can use to craft an impromptu lesson that
will harness energy and engage students?

### Actions

Create a daily formative assessment that provides immediate feedback to students.
Find one lesson that you could shift teacher-delivered content to a peer-to-peer
experience such as a gallery walk or jigsaw activity.

### Go Deeper

Convert all of the direct instruction for one lesson to a student-centered experience
such as a practical use activity, gallery walk, or jigsaw.

# 7

# EVERY STUDENT IS DOING THE BEST THEY CAN RIGHT NOW

**Some hikes are short flat rail-trails, others are days long backpacking excursions.** There is value in both. We must choose the path that is best for us at the time.
⇢ Choosing your path ⇠

## Short Rail Trails: Short Term Goals

One of my first jobs was working in an insurance claims office. I watched the vice president of the small company graciously deal with customer complaints almost every day. One day, I asked her how she could possibly have such a positive attitude toward customers and employees when she dealt with complaints most of the day. Her response is something that has stuck with me. She said,

"No one is trying to do a bad job, everyone is doing the best they can right now." Since then, I have called upon those words of wisdom many times; they have saved me from judgment and aggravation more times than I can count. One thing I'd like to add to her wisdom is if we want people to improve, then we should help them develop the tools and knowledge to do so. Regardless of their current achievement or academic level, we must acknowledge that every kid is doing the best they can with the tools they have right now.

### The Excursions: Keep Your Eyes On The Prize

Have you ever bumped into a challenging student either after graduation or years after they were in your classroom to see that they are successful and happy? Sometimes it is a struggle and sometimes it takes longer than we think it should, but we must be confident that our students will accomplish great things and grow to be healthy happy people eventually.

I had to come to the realization that sometimes biology is not the most important thing in a student's life right now [gasp]. Even with the best of intentions, forcing them to do work on my timeline or reprimanding a student for not being able to be present in class can damage our relationship. I've begun getting to know my students right from the very first day of school. This way I can better understand their behaviors and help them develop the tools they will need to be successful in our class. Tools like collaborating, leading, following directions, using feedback rather than seeing it purely as criticism can be especially difficult for students. One year or semester may not be long enough to gain these skills but every student has the potential to be successful eventually. Every little bit helps.

*Ah-ha moments are okay but I want my students to emerge; to see themselves being successful.*

Some fantastic classroom days are because of ah-ha moments, but many of the best days are the breakthroughs like connecting with difficult to reach students, seeing a struggling student get help from a peer, or watching a quiet or insecure student emerge.

Sometimes, even when I have done everything that I know I can do to provide

- Choices
- Authentic experiences
- Real-world applications
- Empowerment to safely share their learning

students still aren't accomplishing the tasks that I wish they would. When it is taking kids longer than I expected because they are not reaching the goals that I had set for them, or they are distracted and disengaged, I have to realize that every student is doing the best they can right now.

So what does this mean? Is there something else I can do for this particular student? Is there something outside of school that is out of my control keeping this kid from being successful? What does a teacher do when distractions are not in the classroom? When a person is struggling, even small accomplishments feel like something. As teachers, we can create these small accomplishments to intentionally build student confidence. Any assignment can be broken down into smaller chunks for students to complete successfully. The amount of support given to each student will vary. Think of a student who comes to school every day distracted by things that are happening in their life. *They come to school every day.* Every day we have an opportunity to show them what success feels like even if it is just a small win. Let's not dwell on the work that is not being done or the goals that are not being met; we can focus on the positive. It's simple math; adding even small things is better than subtracting.

*It's simple math; adding even small things is better than subtracting.*

Every accomplishment is a step toward a goal. So, when I see these kids that come to our class and just show up but don't get any work done and don't participate in class, I reframe my perspective. I take time to step back and remember that just coming to school is an accomplishment and that this may be the best this kid can do on that day.

One thing we must remind ourselves is that kids aren't giving me a hard time. Kids are having a hard time. It is difficult not to take interactions personally. Teaching is a very personal profession. We are invested in our students, we are passionate about our content, and we want to see everyone being successful. During these times, I remind myself that everyone's success will look different. Everyone's success should look different.

*Kids aren't giving you a hard time.*
*Kids are having a hard time.*

Student-paced milestone projects allow kids to move as quickly or slowly as they choose. Using this model has maximized student success in my classroom; it builds confidence, which transfers into success in other areas. Using a platform like Hyperdocs or Wakelet makes it easier to share a cluster of work with students. I always enjoy seeing the look of accomplishment on a student's face when they finish a task that at first seemed insurmountable. It feels good as a teacher to know that I have accomplished something beyond content knowledge, something much more pervasive that will reach into all aspects of a student's life. I continually reassure kids that it's okay as long as we are not subtracting. The resilience to keep working — even if it is very slow — is an essential life skill.

## Tools For Your Backpack

### Questions

Recall a time when you were overwhelmed. What help did you receive or would you have wanted to receive during that time?

How do kids participate in goal-setting in your classroom?

When have you seen a student struggle because of the amount of work not the difficulty of the work assigned to them?

### Actions

Take one long-term project and break it down into chunks that students can independently manage at their own pace.

Designate a portion of your class time to goal-setting and reflection for students.

### Go Deeper

Investigate some student self-assessment methods at Read Write Think

https://bit.ly/38cWCf8

8

# EVERY STUDENT CAN DO BETTER WITH TIME AND SUPPORT

**Hikers apply what they have learned from short trips to enable them to go on much longer backpacking excursions.** We would not attempt to hike Mt. Everest without training and support.

⇝ Let's find training and support for ambitious goals ⇜

## Everyday Training: Goal-Setting

As I began to reflect on the big picture of years of teaching, I realized there was a flow. There is a difference between short-term and long-term planning, but these things should work together to be most effective. Remember my goal to run a 10K? I did not open my door one day and just run for ten thousand meters. Each day I build a little more stamina and run a couple more meters. Some days I just go for a hike, but I'm never subtracting. Every time I'm putting one foot in front of the other it is practice for my long-term goal of running a 10K.

So, how does this translate to classroom practice? At the beginning of the year, I give students small chunks of work with increasing freedom as they become comfortable with this agency that may be new to them. We practice small goals and celebrate small victories. At first, we celebrate every small step. Eventually, the celebration is not needed; the victory is its own reward. The accomplishment itself is the motivation to keep trying.

Once we realize that everyone is doing their best with their current situation and skills, we must also acknowledge that each student can do better with time and support. It becomes the teacher's responsibility to decide how much time is spent and ultimately, how well each student will do. This is why I like to give students the opportunity to move at different paces. This is not realistic in a teacher-centered class. The decision to decrease my talking time made this clear to me.

This takes quite a bit of planning on my part and doesn't always look the same from one unit to the next, which ideally it would. There are methods that I have found work really well for my students including retrieval practice, projects, reflection, journaling, and hands-on work — demonstrations of learning other than traditional exams, paper and pencil and the digital equivalent. To encourage students to attempt these new methods, I incorporated each one of these as no-stakes opportunities into learning routines.

**Not Every Lesson Will Be A Masterpiece**

One of my favorite musicians is Dave Matthews. During the band's improvisational jams, I become immersed in his music and drift off into thought. The beautiful renditions of classic songs recorded at iconic venues evoke similar yet distinctly different emotions and wonderings each time I listen to them. Try listening to the album version of Ants Marching and the live Summer Tour Warm Up 5.17.13 version for a clear example of how the performance is driven by the enthusiasm of the audience.

Now that you've spent some time reimagining what is possible and how your students will thrive in a culture of curiosity, you may want to jump in with both feet. My advice to you is to not pressure yourself to fully transform every lesson right away. Remember, even Dave Matthews has pop songs. Improvisations are so meaningful because they were created for that particular audience at that moment. Pop songs and scripted lesson plans are reliable and predictable. Sometimes, when the mood strikes us, we should improvise based on the curiosity and wonderings of the students around us to create something powerful and memorable.

## The Power Of Support: PLNs And PBL

By making a change as simple as adding a bathroom sign-out sheet, I was able to figure out that students didn't need me to teach them as much as they needed me to provide the conditions where they can learn.

Some foundational shifts have been:

- Activities that amplify their natural curiosity intrinsically engage students in learning activities instead of listening to me talk them through content and curriculum.
- Grading processes that provide feedback first while creating an environment of nurturing curiosity, collaboration, and multiple attempts at learning.
- Removing zeros and eventually all numerical grades while modeling growth mindset and eliminating academic pressure.

These shifts to my practice were not done because I saw other people do them successfully; they were solutions to problems that I saw in my classroom. I found these solutions accidentally. Then I found the power of the professional learning network.

While no two PLNs are the same, many are similar. If you are looking for a way to build or expand your network, I recommend following hashtags on Twitter. You can do this by conducting a search from your Twitter account or directly in your internet browser search bar. For example, typing #edchat will bring up a variety of Tweets about education-related topics. Starting out following hashtags exposes you to a variety of people and conversations. From there you can decide which ideas and people you want to see more of — or less of. There are Twitter chats that happen at scheduled times either weekly, biweekly, or monthly, but you can participate anytime by searching for the hashtag and responding using the hashtag in your Tweet. Twitter chats are public and anyone can participate or read through the posts and comments. These threads are full of ideas and people that you can connect with by following their accounts.

| General Education Chats | Alternative Grading Chats | Topical Edu Chats |
|---|---|---|
| #edchat | #TG2chat | #2pencilchat |
| #satchat | #masterychat | #crazyPLN |
| #sunchat | #TTOG | #CultureEd |
| #EduGladiators | | #EducationNeverDies |

Podcasts are another powerful tool that I have used to expand my PLN and inspire me to try new things by taking ownership of my classroom climate to make decisions aligned with what I know in my heart is right.

| General Education Podcasts | Leadership Podcasts |
|---|---|
| Cult of Pedagogy | Better Leaders Better Schools |
| Pondering Education | Lead to Succeed |
| Google Teacher Podcast | Leader of Learning |
| Rethink Learning Podcast | School Leadership Series |
| Teachers on Fire | |

Through social media, I found like-minded educators who were struggling with the same difficulties and refused to accept the status quo. Interestingly, many of us independently came up with similar solutions to these problems. If I had connected with these groups sooner, I could have been making changes and improving learning outcomes, and nurturing the love of learning for more students.

The ability to instantly access current, accurate, relevant information from multiple sources means it is no longer necessary for an individual to be an expert of all things. Perhaps the days of "Jack of all trades" or the one guru are behind us and it is time to embrace the collective genius. Technology has made it possible to connect with networks of experts from all fields in real-time. I wanted to use PBL to create a sense of discovery while taking advantage of collective genius.

## Project-Based Learning

Project-based learning engages students in finding meaningful solutions to real-world problems. There are some amazing formal programs where students collaborate with experts outside of the classroom, engineer solutions, and communicate their results. PBLWorks is a great resource (https://www.pblworks.org/) .

In my classroom, it makes more sense to incorporate multiple short-term projects based on student curiosity similar to Genius Hour https://geniushour.com/ or 20time http://www.20time.org/. I was inspired by the work of Don Eckert http://harmonizedlearning. blogspot.com/ to incorporate a modified version of his work into my courses that better fit my semester schedule.

Starting with QFT (described in Chapter 3) at the start of each unit gets kids thinking, wondering, and applying prior learning. From there, students choose which question they want to focus on or which problem they would like to solve. Each student researches their topic of choice using a variety of traditional and non-traditional methods. I facilitate their work by providing resources such as videos, articles, textbook chapters, podcasts, and activities to deepen their understanding. I encourage students to connect with experts via social media and email. We have had scientist guest speakers video conference with us to explain their research. Each unit ends with student presentations and student self-evaluation using the rubric that they created (described in chapter 4).

## Tools For Your Backpack

### Questions

How do you encourage students to reflect on the feedback that you have provided? Think about your routines. Where is there time lost to transitions or ineffective processes? How can you make the most of that time?

### Actions

Find an innovative teacher who is incorporating student-centered learning. Ask them to share ideas or allow you to observe their classroom. Ask a teacher to observe one of your classes. Use a checklist and focus on the mode of instruction, feedback, and downtime.

### Go Deeper

Explore PLNs on Twitter and Facebook. Subscribe to podcasts and blogs.

http://www.letschangeeducation.com/

http://ponderingeducation.com/the-pondering-education-podcast/

# 9

# WOULDN'T IT BE AWESOME IF...

**The hike to the summit of Mt. Washington is an intimidating 6,288 feet of rough terrain, gusting winds, and freezing temperatures.** This is what makes the accomplishment so much sweeter.

⇢ Let's go big ⇠

## Wouldn't It Be Awesome if...My Classroom Experience Truly Matched My Philosophy of Teaching?

I found myself asking this question often until members of my PLN pushed me to make changes that empowered me to do what I knew in my heart was best for kids.

It is because of the support and encouragement of pioneering educational change agents that came before me that I had the courage to disrupt traditional grading practices by using proficiency scales and standards-based reporting. Proficiency scales changed the evaluation and grading conversations that I had with students.

Clearly written proficiency scales shared with students at the introduction of the instructional sequence lead to productive conversations. Bringing students into the conversation helps them become more invested in their learning so they are able to go from "How can I get my grade up?" to

"Can you help me with ___," and

"I'd like to know more about _____."

The scale that I use with students clearly identifies which concepts students are expected to know while leaving out the method of knowledge demonstration. This empowers students to determine for themselves how they will show their learning. These scales also facilitate goal-setting conversations. Once students are familiar with using this type of evaluative tool, each student is able to determine which concepts are essential for them to know personally.

| Exceeds Proficiency | Demonstrates Proficiency | Approaching Proficiency | Limited Proficiency | No Proficiency |
|---|---|---|---|---|
| Independently meets proficiency and is able to make advanced inferences and make authentic connections to _____ | Independently explains the essential concepts of _____. Independently able to identify more complex concepts including _____. | With some help is able to explain all essential concepts of _____ including: _____ | With some help is able to meet some proficiency targets. | With help is unable to explain many of the proficiency targets. |

Feedback on individual assignments is posted in Google Classroom and students are encouraged to revise and resubmit any assignment. Using this platform, students can see their progress, reflect on their learning, and set goals all in one place. Once students have reached the end of a learning sequence, I use the school's grading platform to report required grades to transcripts based on the proficiency scale. This means there are no individual assignments listed on the school's grading platform. The assignment columns in the grading platform are named for the content standard or learning objective.

Now my philosophy of teaching and learning routines are aligned. Students are agents of their own learning. Each student has chosen how they will learn the content and how they will be evaluated. And because I decreased direct instruction to less than 10 percent of class time, I had more time to have meaningful conversations about learning.

## The Accomplishment: Doing Better Things

In order to write *What School Could Be*, Ted Dintersmith (2018) traveled the country visiting schools and speaking to stakeholders. He discussed pockets of excellence all across the United States — individual teachers employing innovative practices and engaging students in deep, meaningful learning activities. He summarized what he found as the difference between doing better things and doing obsolete things better. A school's improved performance on standardized tests did not mean that their students were better prepared for life after graduation. When assessment data was disaggregated, he found that some populations of students were prepared for college exams while others had been overlooked or intentionally side-stepped in the process of racing to the top.

We have students in our classrooms five days a week. Students want to make the most of their day. When every class becomes the same with teacher-centered instruction notes, assignments, worksheets, and homework, students will try to escape either on their phones, leaving the room, or other off-task behaviors. If you simply begin to try doing more engaging and rewarding things, you will find an increase in engagement. Initiate activities that recruit students' interests and histories that will draw students into academic conversations. If you have a variety of lessons that you have used to cover a concept over the years, consider how you might be able to offer each of those as choices for students. These can be your first step toward making a big difference to your students.

Every year I attend our school graduation ceremony. As I watch the graduating class cross the stage, I see my former students collect their diplomas as the officiator of the graduation announces each student's post-secondary plan. I see my former students announcing that they are going to biotechnology, veterinary, medical, and other life science-based pathways. Perhaps lessons that employed their interests and empowered them to expand on them had something to do with that.

Recall the Twain quote from Chapter 2. The day you find out why you were born. There have been many of these for me. There was a time when I was sure that my purpose in life was to be a scientist. Through my life experiences and my learned willingness to be flexible, I have discovered that my purpose in life is continually evolving. Having a stalwart vision of the pathway to my purpose has not always served me well. Much of what I have accomplished in my life has been the result of my willingness to be flexible. As I have worked to write this book, I have found a new sharper focus on what I need to do to fulfill myself. I will continue to focus on science and advocating for science education, and perhaps being a laboratory scientist was never my calling. Inspiring a generation of students is where I am right now; maybe inciting change through supporting educators will help me fulfill that purpose.

I think back to the kindergarten sheet where I decided that I wanted to be a teacher. The choices that I was presented with had no impact on my decision to be a teacher. I had no experience with preschool or daycare; I was a teacher before I even knew what a teacher was. This is the passion that we must keep alive in our students. Let's also consider the options that kindergarten sheet presented to me; mother, nurse, airline hostess, model, secretary, or teacher. The gender bias is undeniable and the choices are ridiculous. Frankly, the entire activity is flawed starting with the question. Let's not ask kids what they want to be when they grow up. Let's ask them what problem they want to solve and help them set goals that will lead them toward that target. Let us then devise experiences that will give them the knowledge that will empower them to realize their goals and opportunities to self-evaluate and refocus.

*If you keep doing the
same old things;
you are going to keep getting the
same results.*

What I have done is to create opportunities to act on ideas that many teachers have shared with me. Make no mistake, these opportunities were not given; I did not wait for permission. I did it on my own with the support of my professional learning networks. In my relatively brief experience as a teacher, I have found that some of my peers shy away from innovative practices due to several factors including fear of failure and lack of support. If not for my professional learning networks, the changes that I made would have taken much longer. I have also found that even the most tried-and-true practices can fail and support is all around us so try something new!

Students appreciate teachers who try new things and encourage them to think differently in the classroom and beyond. My hope is that this book encourages you to find a supportive PLN that will give you the courage to pursue your own greatness and share it with the world.

## Tools For Your Backpack

### Questions

Are your expectations limiting what you can accomplish?
How might your expectations be limiting what your students can accomplish?
What can you incorporate into your unit plans to regularly encourage students to consider interests that they may never have been exposed to?

### Actions

Revisit your "why" and unpack all the reasons that you became a teacher.

### Go Deeper

Research FedEx Days and 20% time for teachers and students.
Daniel Pink's blog http://bit.ly/PinkFedEx
20 Time.org http://www.20time.org/

# 10

# THE 6TH E "EMPOWER"

Once a person has achieved a goal that they once thought was out of their reach, they are confident and feel empowered to set even higher goals for themselves.

➤ Let's empower ourselves to achieve greatness ↤

## We All Have Something to Teach

In order to prepare students for the state standardized test, I give them a copy of a previous version of the test. Instead of grading them on their performance, after they have completed the test, I give them the answers. Their job is to teach one another strategies they have learned to choose the right answer and reflect on why they have gotten an answer incorrect. I have seen students describe the traditional "eliminate one option tactic" and describing the importance of recalling lessons from class that help them to remember the concept that is being covered in the question. We call this activity, "You teach the class." What I have found is that this empowers students to see themselves as teachers and to see these intimidating high stakes tests as an opportunity to learn.

## We All Have Something To Learn

Another powerful thing that I have realized is that we all have something to learn. I learn something new every single day. Sometimes it comes from unexpected sources. Now I welcome the opportunity to learn from anyone anywhere, formally or informally. I learn from my students every day about empathy, patience, resilience, and even science.

## The Writer

A notable example of this is the student who was looking for an opportunity to practice writing. She loved science and she loved creative writing. Instead of being required to produce all of the technical writing of a traditional science class, I gave her the freedom to choose something she would enjoy writing. The result was the story of Sara Little-Turnbull. I'm guessing that most people reading this do not know Sara Little-Turnbull. Neither did I. What I learned from my student is that this woman who worked at 3M in the early 1900s is responsible for the design of the N95 face mask that has been so important during the COVID-19 pandemic. The student's work was eloquently and thoughtfully written. In it, she expressed the challenges that women in the workplace faced in the 1900s and how Sara became a successful businesswoman and designer. Her research essay was submitted and published in a peer-reviewed journal before she graduated high school!

## We Can All Achieve Greatness!

In 1987, the Biological Sciences Curriculum Study (BSCS) developed the widely used 5E instructional model. This model starts with engagement, providing students with some hook while assessing the prior knowledge of individual students. The lesson proceeds through engagement, exploration, explanation, extension, and finally evaluation.

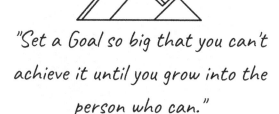

"Set a Goal so big that you can't achieve it until you grow into the person who can."

I propose a 6th E, empowerment. By mistakes, observing, reflecting, and taking action, I have discovered ways that students can be empowered to ask and investigate questions, share learning and curiosities with their classmates and a larger audience at any of these stages. These learning adventures culminate with a public display of knowledge.

**You can eradicate "why do I have to learn this" from your classroom with the 6th E!**

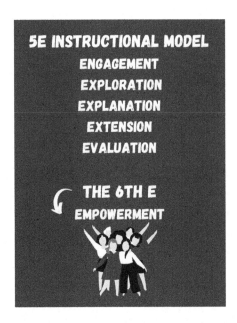

Empowerment means supporting students to become what they want while providing guidance and encouraging them to dream bigger. Ah-Ha moments are not enough; even the prioritization of building classroom communities sometimes falls short of empowering students to reach for their loftiest goals.

*"Whoever teaches learns in the act of teaching,*
*and whoever learns teaches in the act of learning."*
*Paulo Freire*

**Empower Learning Outside of Classroom Walls**

StartEdUp Foundation (www.startedupinnovation.com) started as a 20% time project in Don Wettrick's classroom. His process inspired students to develop entrepreneurial mindsets through his process of coaching innovation, encouraging students to collaborate with mentors outside of school, and embrace failure. This led him and his students to start a nonprofit that supports other teachers and students who do the same.

### Reaching The Summit: Looking Back at Progress

Finally, after years of reflection and pushing boundaries, I have aligned my idea of what learning should be with what teaching actually is. By translating my simple observations into action I have:

- Increased student agency.
- Increased student-centered instruction.
- Empowered students to choose how they want to demonstrate knowledge.
- Empowered students to choose how they want to acquire knowledge.
- Coached students through acting on feedback to keep moving forward.
- Coached students through the process of defining what learning looks like for them personally.
- Coached students through the process of thoughtfully evaluating their own progress toward self-defined goals.

What began as a disjointed view of teaching and learning evolved into using reflection to:

- Increase formative assessment to inform instruction and quickly pivot.
- Decrease teacher-centered instruction to <10% of class while maintaining structured routines that provide Choices, Authentic experiences, Real-world applications, and Empowerment to share their learning outside of the classroom.

- Developed routines that meaningfully connect learning to student real-life experiences and interests.
- Align teaching and learning that empowers every single student every single day.

## Tools for Your Backpack

### Questions

How can you use inactive time to build a community culture in your classroom? In what ways can you support students that are passionate about something where you have no expertise?

### Actions

Encourage students to share their passions with you. Connect them with an organization that will help to amplify their work.

### Go Deeper

Check out StartEdUp.

http://www.startedupinnovation.com/

# CONCLUSION

As I look back on my years of experience, I cannot pinpoint a single moment where I thought I was doing something that would transform teaching and learning in my classroom. I have never been concerned about upholding traditions for their own sake; I've looked for opportunities to research and try new things. Perhaps you have a similar experience or want to make changes to your classroom routine and culture that will increase student engagement and achievement.

It has sometimes been challenging for me to convince students that taking risks will pay off; that shifting their mindsets from the traditional academic cycle of lecture quiz homework test repeat will ultimately lead to greater success. Once it does happen, the energy is infectious. Taking the first step toward creating a student-centered learning space requires courage, but when you have, you will see a marked difference in student behavior and engagement. Colleagues may become curious about what you are doing differently and they, too, will begin to break free of the assessment cycle that no longer serves our students.

There is not one "best practice" to make every student successful. Instead, I have shared several activities that can be incorporated into your routines to foster agency by providing choices, authentic experiences, real-world applications, that empower every student every day.

Learning can and should be enjoyable. While challenging, it should never be stressful and students should never feel pressured to cheat rather than use mistakes as opportunities to learn. You can create a classroom community that makes school a place where every kid knows they were appreciated and supported while providing work that is academically rigorous and rewarding.

# REFERENCES

Dintersmith, T. (2018). What school could be: Insights and inspiration from teachers across America. Princeton, NJ: Princeton University Press.

Heath, C. (2018). Power of moments: Why certain experiences have extraordinary impact. New York, NY: Simon and Schuster.

Pink, D. (2013). Drive: The surprising truth about what motivates us. New York, NY:. Riverhead Books.

Spall, T. (2018, October 01). Teaching tip Thursday: Digital menu for student creation. Retrieved from https://brenhamtechdaily.blogspot.com/2017/10/teaching-tip-thursday-digital-menu-for.html/

# ABOUT THE AUTHOR

Bonnie Nieves has over a decade of experience as a high school Biology teacher. She has a Master's Degree in Curriculum and Instruction and Educational Leadership. She is passionate about creating immersive and authentic experiences that fuel curiosity and creating student-centered, culturally responsive learning spaces that promote equity and inclusion. She is a Google Level 2 certified educator and serves on the MassCUE board of directors. She enjoys connecting with educators through social media, professional organizations, conferences, Twitter chats, and edcamps. Bonnie is also a member of the National Association of Biology Teachers, Teacher

Institute for Evolutionary Science, and National Science Teaching Association and founder of the Educate On Purpose community. She encourages you to connect with her on Twitter @biologygoddess, Instagram @beawesomeonpurpose, Clubhouse @biologygoddess, and LinkedIn.

Please visit www.educateonpurpose.com and www.beawesomeonpurpose.org for information about her current projects.

Made in United States
North Haven, CT
18 May 2022